A book
is a present you can open
again and again.

THIS BOOK BELONGS TO

_____

FROM

_____

A <u>Forest</u> Tree House

Written by Sheryl A. Reda

Illustrated by Peter Barrett

TREASURE TREE ™

World Book, Inc.
a Scott Fetzer company
Chicago   London   Sydney   Toronto

Printed in the United States of America
ISBN 0-7166-1619-X
Library of Congress Catalog Card No. 91-65750

B/IB

Cover design by Rosa Cabrera
Book design by George Wenzel

Do you think that it would be fun to live underground or in a tree? Maybe you would like it for a little while. But for the creatures that live in the forest, those places are just right all the time.

The woodland oak stands strong and tall.
A gentle breeze rustles through its leaves.
"Thissss . . . Thissss," the leaves seem to say as
they sway. Except for the leaves, everything
about the oak seems still and quiet. Nothing
else is stirring. Or is it?

Look closely at the catkins. These are the
flowery tassels that swing and sway with the
rustling leaves. Some "catkins" are not catkins
at all! They're caterpillars. They look like the
catkins, so it's hard for you to see them. More
important, it's hard for animals that eat insects
to see them. This is the insects' protection.

A green katydid perches on a leaf. What
part of the tree does it look like? Find the
walking stick insect, too. Its legs look like
twigs. Where is the best place for it to hide?

Rat-a-tat-tat. *Rat-a-tat-tat*. The insects sense danger. Is it a squirrel or a gray fox shaking things up? No. It's a woodpecker that lives in a hole in the tree. He's not tapping on the tree to make music. He hammers on the tree because he's hunting for bark-boring beetles and their young grubs. That's what he eats. His special beak helps him get to the grubs deep inside the tree bark.

The caterpillar, katydid, and walking stick
are not afraid of the woodpecker. He's not
interested in eating them. They are safe—until
they hear the vireo songbird singing. He sings
sweetly to his mate as she returns to their
treetop nest. Vireos eat all kinds of insects.

Other birds live in the tree, too. Can you
see the ovenbirds way down below? Ovenbirds
hide their nest on the forest floor.

A hawklike cry shatters the quiet. The
birds look up expectantly. Uh-oh. It's a blue
jay. He has the same cry as a hawk. He has
come to rob their nests. The ovenbird and
vireos must act quickly. They flap their wings
boldly and shout and scold the blue jay.
Discouraged, the blue jay flies off. He's going
to find an unprotected nest to rob. The vireos
and ovenbirds can relax now.

Unlike blue jays, the red-shouldered hawks who live in the oak are friendly neighbors. They may even share their nests with sparrows.

Hawks are hunters, and they eat many kinds of animals. They prey on mice, moles, snakes, fish, and insects.

A mole makes its home near the oak. It dug a tunnel underground. Like all moles, this one is very quick and very shy. It will only venture out to hunt for the insects it eats for food.

The chipmunk burrows under the oak, too. But it spends time outside its hole. It scurries around gathering nuts and seeds. It stashes them in pouches in its cheeks. When the pouches are full, the chipmunk's face looks fat and round.

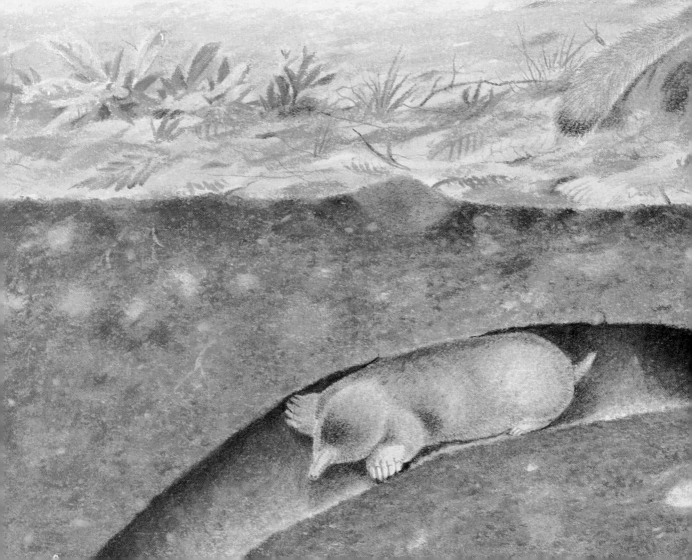

A black rat snake makes its home in the oak. When it senses danger, it slithers off into the safety of a crack or hole in the tree. Do you see any other good hiding places for the black rat snake? If the black rat snake can't get away fast enough, it has another way of protecting itself. It can shake its tail like a poisonous rattlesnake. That frightens whatever is frightening it!

This wood duck will nest in a tree hole high inside the oak until her chicks are hatched. Meanwhile, she must protect her nest from the black rat snake and other animals. Before she goes off to get a meal of acorns, she covers her nest with twigs, grass, and leaves. This keeps her eggs safe and warm. Once her eggs hatch, she will lead her family to the pond. They will make a new home in the shallow pond water.

Soon after the ducks leave, squirrels take over the nest. All summer long, squirrels have lived in an open tree nest. But summer doesn't last forever. Why would the old duck nest be a good winter home?

Squirrels scamper around the forest as if they own it! They look for acorns, nuts, seeds, and fruit. They need a lot of food. But they won't eat it all now. Squirrels store food so that they will have something to eat through the winter.

The squirrel must be cautious when he is on the ground. Some of his neighbors, such as the red fox, are a threat.

The red foxes have a roomy den in the oak, down beneath the tree's roots. Now that the cubs are almost grown, the whole family hunts together. Foxes eat insects, frogs, birds, and other small prey besides squirrels. The squirrel is safe now though, because red foxes don't climb trees!

Raccoons are tree climbers, but this one isn't looking for squirrels. He wants the honey that the bees make in their hive. To get the honey, the raccoon has to claw his way up the tree and snatch it away from the bees. But then he has to hurry down because the angry bees are on the way! Raccoons' thick fur protects them against bee stings.

White tail deer visit the oak. They nibble
on the leaves and rest in the shade. Like all the
creatures who live in and around the oak, the
deer are always on their guard. They need to
be alert against enemies. At the first hint of
danger, they dart away.

Soon the forest will seem empty and
quiet again. But you know better—the forest
is always teeming with life. Shhh . . . let's not
disturb.

Who Lives Where?

This oak tree is home to all sorts of animals. Can you match each of the animals below with its forest home?

Hint: Remember, the wood duck and squirrel could be using the same home—at different times!

More About Curious Forest Creatures

The male red-eyed vireo knows more than 40 different songs. Whenever he sings, he varies his style from song to song.

Chipmunks, squirrels, and other rodents have to gnaw on things. If they didn't, their teeth would grow to be so long that they couldn't chew anything.

Katydids, like crickets, sing by rubbing their front wings together. What's more unusual is that they hear with their knees. That's where their eardrums are.

Snakes smell with the tips of their forked tongues. They touch their tongues to an organ in the roof of their mouths.

Squirrels don't remember where they bury their food. They have to sniff the ground for clues.

A red fox's den may have many entrances.

To Parents

Children delight in hearing and reading about birds and other small creatures. *A Forest Tree House* will provide your child with interesting information about a number of these, as well as a bridge into learning some important concepts. Here are a few easy and natural ways your child can express feelings and understandings about the animals in the book. You know your child and can best judge which ideas he or she will enjoy most.

Your child may be familiar with many of the creatures in the book, and you can have fun singing together about them. Use the tune from the song "Old MacDonald Had a Farm." Change the words to "The large forest had a tree, . . . and in this tree there lived a [animal's name]."

Are there any birds living in your neighborhood? If so, you can help your child make them a bird feeder. First mix equal parts of peanut butter and corn meal. Roll a pine cone in this mixture and then in bird seed. Hang your feeder outside where your child can watch the birds come to eat.

Flowering plants can add color to your home, and they attract lovely creatures such as ladybugs and butterflies. Your child may enjoy starting a garden indoors. Help fill some paper cups with soil and then plant a seed in each one. Remind your child to water the garden. When the plants are tall enough, replant them outside in garden pots or flower beds. Watch to see who comes visiting!

Squirrels, birds, and other small nest-building animals might appreciate your child's help. Give your child a mesh onion bag and help stuff it with brightly colored yarn scraps, or fabric or paper strips. Pull the pieces through the holes so that the birds can get at them. Place the bag outside and watch for several days to see if any animals take the materials for their nests. Your child might even see a piece in a nest.

A forest-creature chart can help your child discover how forest animals are alike and different. Across the top of a piece of paper, have your child write *Birds*, *Insects*, and *Furry Animals*. Then help your child name the creatures in the book and list each creature in the correct column.